THE HEYDAY OF THE **PEAKS**

Gavin Morrison

Ian Allan
PUBLISHING

Front cover: During August 1959 pioneering BR/Sulzer Type 4 No D1 was transferred to Camden depot to take up duties on the West Coast main line, although it had previously visited Carlisle Citadel station on 14 July 1959 to be named *Scafell Pike*. It is seen here near Berkswell at the head of the 2.40pm Euston–Manchester Piccadilly express, diverted via Coventry, on 18 June 1961, during its second spell at Camden. After moving to Longsight, it would (along with the rest of its class) settle at Toton in February 1962, following which date the original 'Peaks' would seldom be seen on passenger duties. Renumbered 44 001, this historic locomotive would be withdrawn in October 1976 and cut up in February 1977. *M. Mensing*

Back cover: On 10 August 1985, having worked the overnight Glasgow Central–Bristol Temple Meads sleeper from Birmingham New Street, No 45 142 (D83) removes the sleeping cars before returning to work the rest of the train as a service to the West Country. This locomotive was to meet its end on 18 June 1987, when it caught fire at Slaithwaite, leading to its eventual withdrawal. *Gavin Morrison*

Previous page: In the days when there were enough football fans to justify running a Footex for a special game No 45 023 (ex-D54) *The Royal Pioneer Corps* leaves Halifax with 'Town' supporters bound for Sheffield on 12 April 1982. This locomotive was loaned to Willington power station for a month in 1968, and set a world record of 341 hours' non-stop engine running during its visit. It would be withdrawn on 12 September 1984 and cut up by Vic Berry of Leicester during November 1986. *Gavin Morrison*

First published 2005

ISBN 0 7110 3057 X

Published by Ian Allan Publishing

an imprint of Ian Allan Publishing Ltd, Hersham, Surrey KT12 4RG.
Printed in England by Ian Allan Printing Ltd, Hersham, Surrey KT12 4RG.

Code: 0504/B

Below: Ready for conducting trials on the London Midland Region, brand-new No D1 stands outside Derby Works on 25 May 1959. It carries *Scafell Pike* nameplates, although the official ceremony, at Carlisle station, would not take place until 14 July. As No 44 001 the locomotive would remain in service until October 1976, being cut up the following February. *R. C. Riley*

Introduction

British Railways' Modernisation Plan of 1955 envisaged a 'Pilot Scheme' whereby an initial 20 diesel-electric locomotives would be constructed in the Type C (later Type 4) category of 2,000+hp. Of these, 10 were ordered from English Electric (materialising as Nos D200-9), but the remaining 10 were to be built at BR's own workshops at Derby. The latter design was based largely on that produced by the LMS for its prototype diesels (Nos 10000/1) of 1947/8 but utilised the 12-cylinder 'A'-series Sulzer LDA engine, manufactured in Switzerland and developing a maximum of 2,300hp, while the generator and traction motors were produced by Crompton-Parkinson at Chelmsford. Maximum tractive effort was initially 70,000lb, but this was reduced to 50,000. However, weight was significantly greater than that of the LMS diesels, and to keep within a 20-ton maximum axle loading it was necessary to adopt the

cumbersome 1Co-Co1 wheel arrangement of the three SR-designed prototypes (Nos 10201-3). Frames for the first example were laid in August 1958, the locomotive duly emerging in April 1959 as No D1 *Scafell Pike* and turning the scales at 133 tons 3cwt.

The class was completed in February 1960 with the delivery of No D10 *Tryfan*, all 10 locomotives being named after mountain peaks in England or Wales, from which they became known as 'Peaks'. All were based initially at Camden depot,

from which they were employed on the West Coast main line, working expresses as far north as Perth. When new No D2 *Helvellyn* was fitted with an engine uprated to 2,500hp and as such was used on high-speed trials to test the track condition prior to the introduction of the electrics; its gearing was modified so that it could exceed its official 90mph maximum, and 110mph was achieved with three coaches.

British Rail was under pressure to eliminate steam, to such an extent that in the spring of 1957, before trials with the

Seen nearing completion inside Derby Works on the same day, No D2 has its *Helvellyn* nameplate already fitted. The 10 Pilot Scheme 'Peaks' (later Class 44) were fitted with 2,300hp 12-cylinder Sulzer engines, although No D2 would later be fitted with an uprated (2,500hp) engine; it ran in this form whilst working from Camden depot between September 1959 and July 1961, being used on Euston–Liverpool Lime Street services and tested at 100mph prior to the introduction of the electrics. Having reverted to 2,300hp it spent most of its remaining career on Toton–Whitemoor coal trains, as did the rest of its class. Renumbered 44 002, it would be withdrawn in February 1979 and scrapped in October of that year. *R. C. Riley*

Pilot Scheme locomotives could be completed, an order was placed for a further 137 (later reduced to 127). These were designated mixed-traffic locomotives, a maximum of 90mph with 'B'-series Sulzer engines producing a maximum power output of 2,500hp and 55,000lb tractive effort. Construction was shared between Derby and Crewe Works, the original intention being that Derby should build Nos D11-67 and Crewe Nos D68-137, but the construction of Nos D50–67 was later transferred to Crewe.

Unlike Nos D1-10 these production locomotives (later Class 45) were unnamed when new, and although a number would later be named — mostly after army regiments (some of the names in question having previously been carried by LMS 'Patriot' or 'Royal Scot' steam locomotives) — they too became known as 'Peaks'.

In 1959 a final order was placed for 76 Sulzer-powered Type 4s, all to be built at Derby but with electrical equipment supplied by Brush of Loughborough, (although in the event it was decided to reduce this order by 20 in favour of a completely new Brush/Sulzer design, later Class 47). The first example of what would later become known as Class 46 appeared in November 1960 as No D138, the order being completed with the delivery of No D193 in January 1963 — six months before No D67 emerged from Crewe, fitted with the more powerful (2,750hp) 'C'-series Sulzer engine, to serve as a testbed for the new Brush design.

With electrification of the West Coast main line as far as Crewe it was decided

Above: Very early days for 'Peaks' at Leeds. No D31, which had been on loan to Neville Hill for just three weeks when this picture was taken on 27 June 1961, waits to take over the down 'Thames–Clyde Express' at Leeds City as a locally based Fairburn 2-6-4T prepares to depart for Bradford Forster Square. Renumbered 45 030, the Type 4 diesel would remain allocated to Leeds until October 1977, ultimately being withdrawn from Tinsley on 30 November 1980 and cut up by May 1981. *Gavin Morrison*

Right: A view of Leeds Holbeck depot on 23 March 1967, featuring No D173 (later No 46 036). Note the red buffer-beam and the slightly lighter shade of blue than was used subsequently. Withdrawn in May 1982 as a result of fire damage sustained at Rotherham on 23 April, this locomotive would be scrapped by January 1983. *Gavin Morrison*

to concentrate the 'Peaks' on the Midland main line. Nos D11-137 were soon dominating passenger services between St Pancras and Manchester/Nottingham, together with freight diagrams and as early as 1961 established themselves north of Leeds on expresses to Glasgow via the Settle–Carlisle line. They would later be joined on the Midland Division by the 10 Pilot Scheme locomotives; stripped of their steam-heating boilers and reallocated to Toton in 1962, Nos D1-10 would never again be regularly diagrammed for passenger work, being generally confined to Toton–Whitemoor coal traffic. By contrast Nos D138-93 were used mainly on the East Coast main line and North East–South West services but were not usually seen west of Bristol until the WR's 'Warship' diesel-hydraulics started to be withdrawn in the late 1960s.

As built all 'Peaks' had been fitted with boilers, to enable them to heat carriage stock that originated in the steam era. A significant development in the early 1970s was the fitting of electric train heating (ETH) to 50 members of the D11-137 series (by now minus the 'D' and known as Class 45) for services on the Midland main line; these locomotives were worked hard, their diagrams covering 750-1,000 miles per day, Toton depot carrying out extra maintenance on these locomotives. Around this time BR decided to renumber its locomotive fleet in line with the Total Operations Processing System (TOPS) devised in the late 1960s. First to be addressed was Class 45, locomotives being renumbered rather haphazardly in the order

in which they visited main works; those that retained boilers for steam heating were renumbered in the series 45 001-077 (being thereafter known as Class 45/0), while the ETH examples became 45 101-150 (Class 45/1). The Class 46s were dealt with more logically, being renumbered 46 001-056 in order of construction, while the 10 original locomotives (by now Class 44) similarly became Nos 44 001-010.

'Peak' withdrawals began in July 1976, when No 44 003 was taken out of service, but, a handful of accident victims aside, Classes 45 and 46 remained intact until the 1980s. By this time, however, a general downturn in traffic (particularly freight) was dictating the large-scale withdrawal of surplus diesel locomotives; of the 'Peaks' it was decided that, following elimination of the Class 44s, the Class 46s should go next, and the last of these was withdrawn from

normal service in the spring of 1984. The Class 45/0s were also vulnerable, but for the ETH-fitted '45/1s' the future was somewhat brighter; largely displaced from their Midland main-line duties by HSTs in October 1982, they began to wander all over the network from Penzance to Glasgow. By 1986 they were concentrated on trans-Pennine expresses, but the 'DMU revolution' of the mid-1980s was to strip them of even these duties and lead to their

ultimate withdrawal. The last example to be overhauled was No 45 118 at Derby in 1986, and what was expected to be the final run was made by No 45 141 on a Sheffield–Leeds service in August 1988. No 45 106 was later reinstated and repainted green for special workings (although it did work regular services), but this use was short-lived, for it caught fire near West Hampstead on a down express and was withdrawn on 20 February 1989. No 45 128 was considered as a replacement, but the cost involved put paid to the idea.

Thus came to an end the service career of the 193 'Peaks', which many drivers considered the best of the Sulzer-powered locomotives, especially the Class 45/0s, which seemed to haul their 12-coach trains over the South Devon banks with ease, while the gradients of the Settle–Carlisle

were hardly noticed with the slightly lighter loads. The 1Co-Co1 wheel arrangement nevertheless led to persistent bogie problems, with consequent expense; although specialist welding techniques employed at Toton and carried out by a company called 'Surelock' were successful, the cost involved and the eventual transfer of the class to Tinsley ended the work. In their latter years providing welcome variety from the dominance of the Class 47s, the Class 45s and 46s were extremely popular with the enthusiasts, and fortunately Nos 45 112 and 46 035 can still be seen occasionally on the main line, while others are active on preserved lines.

I should like to conclude by expressing my thanks to those photographers who had the good sense to point their cameras at the green 'Peaks' (at a time when I was

concentrating my efforts on the dwindling numbers of steam locomotives), thereby covering the gaps in my collection. The pictures selected are intended to portray the 'Peaks' on the type of traffic they hauled and the areas in which they worked, and I hope the reader will derive enjoyment from the result.

Gavin Morrison
Mirfield
November 2004

Bibliography
Sulzer Diesel Locomotives of British Rail
 by Brian Webb (David & Charles, 1978)
The Allocation History of BR diesels and Electrics,
 Part 2 by Roger Harris (published by the author
 in 2002)

Left: A returning excursion from Birmingham to York made up of a fine set of InterCity coaches negotiates the crossovers at Monk Fryston, headed by Tinsley-allocated No 45 121 (ex-D18), unofficially named 'Pegasus', on 13 August 1987. The locomotive was derailed at Healey Mills two months after this picture was taken and withdrawn on 19 November 1987, finally being cut up in September 1993 at Derby. *Gavin Morrison*

Right: Until 1988 No 45 106 (ex-D106) was just another ordinary ETH-fitted Class 45 /1, but in the summer of that year Tinsley depot painted it in green livery, and it became a 'celebrity' locomotive. It is shown here on 21 January 1989 ready to leave Leeds City on an InterCity charter over the Settle–Carlisle line, the train having arrived behind the unique Class 89 electric. Unfortunately the 'Peak' was to catch fire near West Hampstead on 3 February, being withdrawn as a result. Consideration was given to painting No 45 128 green as a replacement, but in the event this did not happen. *Gavin Morrison*

Left: After the end of steam on the Midland main line in the early 1960s the 2,500hp BR/Sulzer Type 4s (later Class 45) dominated services until the arrival of the HSTs in October 1982, and in the intervening period it was commonplace to see several 'Peaks' lined up under the famous St Pancras roof, at the head of down expresses. No 45 115 is on the left with the 18.01 to Sheffield and No 45 102 on the right with the 17.16 to Nottingham on 6 May 1978. This fine uninterrupted view of the famous London terminus has now been blocked by the Channel Tunnel Rail Terminal building. *Gavin Morrison*

Above: In fine evening light No 45 110 (ex-D73) passes the impressive signal gantries at Brent Junction No 1 'box in North London with the 17.01 departure from St Pancras to Sheffield on 21 May 1977. Given the unofficial name of 'Medusa' at Tinsley in August 1987, the locomotive would be withdrawn on 27 July 1988, being cut up at MC Metal Processing, Glasgow, on 13 June 1990. *Gavin Morrison*

Left: Green-liveried No D56 (later No 45 137), named *The Bedfordshire and Hertfordshire Regiment (TA)* at Bedford station on 8 December 1962, emerges from Ampthill Tunnel, south of Bedford, at the head of the 11.15 Bradford Forster Square–St Pancras on 20 June 1965. Remaining in service until 15 June 1987, the locomotive would then be stored at March depot for more than six years, finally being sent by road for scrapping at MC Metal Processing, Glasgow, in February 1994. *M. Mensing*

Above: No 45 112 (ex-D61) *The Royal Army Ordnance Corps* heads an afternoon express for St Pancras non-stop through Kettering on 16 August 1980; note the fine platform canopies. The locomotive would be withdrawn on 7 May 1987, remaining derelict at March until sold to the East Lancashire Railway in 1991 for preservation. Re-sold to Fragonset Railways in June 1999, it is currently in full main-line working order. *Gavin Morrison*

Left: Due to engineering work on Saturday 28 June 1986, Nottingham and Sheffield workings were diverted away from the Leicester area via Melton Mowbray, Morton and Corby. Here an afternoon Nottingham–St Pancras express, double-headed by Nos 45 145 and 45 110, rejoins its booked route at Glendon Junction. *Gavin Morrison*

Above: Another picture of a diverted up express on 28 June 1986, this time the 10.30 Nottingham–St Pancras, seen passing through Melton Mowbray station; the train will take the right-hand line at Manton Junction and head for Corby, crossing the famous Harringworth Viaduct. The locomotive is No 45 120 (ex-D107), which like most of the Class 45 /1s would end its working days allocated to Tinsley; withdrawn on 24 March 1987, it would not be broken up until May 1993, at MC Metals, Glasgow. *Gavin Morrison*

13

Above: In the days when there were many fine signal gantries around Leicester, No 45 121 (ex-D18) passes Belle Lane, just to the north of Leicester station, at the head of the 17.10 Sheffield–St Pancras on 29 May 1978. Latterly given the unofficial name of 'Pegasus' by Tinsley depot, the locomotive would be withdrawn in November 1987 as a result of damage sustained in a derailment in Healey Mills yard on 28 October. It would nevertheless remain largely intact as late as March 1993, when it was used for a controlled collision with a Class 158 DMU at BREL Litchurch Lane, Derby, finally being cut up in September 1993. *Gavin Morrison*

Right: A different viewpoint from the usual pictures taken at Loughborough shows ex-works No 45 147 (originally D41) about to pass under the ex-Great Central main-line bridge at the south end of the station, with an afternoon express for St Pancras on 29 May 1978. On 4 December 1984, whilst hauling the 10.05 Liverpool–Scarborough express, this locomotive would be involved in a dramatic crash, ploughing into the back of the 09.00 Stanlow–Leeds tanker train stopped at a signal right alongside the M602 motorway near Eccles. Tragically the ensuing fire resulted in the death of two passengers as well as the premature withdrawal of the locomotive, the latter being cut up at Patricroft in March 1985. *Gavin Morrison*

Left: A study of No 44 010 (ex-D10), minus its *Tryfan* nameplates, standing outside Toton depot — its home for most of its life — on 8 July 1976. Withdrawn on 18 September 1976, this locomotive would be reinstated the following month but withdrawn again on 26 May 1977 after catching fire at Mansfield Junction, ultimately being cut up in July 1978. *Gavin Morrison*

Below left: Although allocated to Cricklewood at the time, Class 45/0 No 45 044 (ex-D63) is seen on shed at Toton depot on 8 July 1976. Named *Royal Inniskilling Fusilier* in January 1965, it would be withdrawn on 15 June 1987 and stored at various sites around the country before being cut up at MC Metal Processing in Glasgow during February 1989. *Gavin Morrison*

Right: Class 46 No 46 054 (ex-D191) takes the London line out of Derby with an unidentified up passenger working on 5 August 1978. The Class 46s were normally used on the cross-country route to Birmingham, and this locomotive spent the majority of its working days allocated to Gateshead. Withdrawn in December 1980 but reinstated in November the following year, it would be withdrawn permanently in January 1982, although not cut up until August 1983. *Gavin Morrison*

Above: No 45 144 (ex-D55) *Royal Signals* powers the 17.10 Sheffield–St Pancras away from Chesterfield on 8 May 1982. It would be withdrawn due to a derailment at Malago Vale carriage sidings, Bristol, on 27 December 1987, although not actually cut up until July 1988, at Vic Berry's yard. *Gavin Morrison*

Right: The footbridge just to the north of Chesterfield station provides a good vantage-point from which to photograph trains. No 45 111 (ex-D65) *Grenadier Guardsman* pulls away from the station with an early-morning

St Pancras–Sheffield as No 45 114 (ex-No D94) approaches with an up working from Sheffield on 5 May 1979. Although withdrawn in May 1987 No 45 111 would not be cut up until July 1992, having been stored in several locations and made available for tests by the Railway Technical Centre at Derby. No 45 114 would end its working days on 17 February 1987, remaining at Whitemoor yard for seven years before being cut up by MC Metal Processing, Glasgow, in February 1994. *Gavin Morrison*

Left: The Summer Saturdays-only 08.27 Bradford–Paignton passes Millhouses on the 1-in-100 climb from Sheffield Midland to the summit in Bradway Tunnel on 13 August 1983. The locomotive is No 45 014 (ex-D137) *The Cheshire Regiment*, named at Chester station on 12 June 1966. It would be withdrawn following a collision with Class 31 No 31 436 at Chinley on 9 March 1986 and cut up at Vic Berry's of Leicester between 19 and 21 August 1986. *Gavin Morrison*

Above: On 2 July 1966, when the Midland main line between Normanton and Sheffield via Royston and Cudworth was still quadruple-track, No D99 (later No 45 135) *3rd Carabinier* heads the up 'Waverley' (Edinburgh–London St Pancras) past Walton, near Wakefield. The old Midland route north from Sheffield is now truncated at Royston and reduced to single-track. Withdrawn in May 1987, the locomotive would be sold in March 1989 for preservation by Peak Rail at Buxton but is now owned by the Pioneer Diesel Group and can be found on the East Lancashire Railway. *Gavin Morrison*

After the closure of the ex-Midland Railway main line between Oakenshaw and Normanton (Goose Hill), Sheffield–Leeds trains were diverted off the Midland main line at Walton, past the site of the old Lancashire & Yorkshire Railway steam shed (on the left of the picture), to Wakefield Westgate and thence to Leeds. No 45 075 (ex-D132) passes Wakefield Belle Vue with a Paignton–Leeds train on 27 July 1976. This locomotive would be withdrawn on 25 January 1985, thereafter spending some time in store at Goole Docks before being cut up at Vic Berry's of Leicester by April 1987. *Gavin Morrison*

This picture was taken on the approach to Oakenshaw, on the outskirts of Wakefield, on the section of the old Midland main line from Normanton (Goose Hill). An immaculate No 45 013 (ex-D20), for several years a Leeds Holbeck locomotive but by now allocated to Tinsley, heads south on 3 May 1987 with a Newcastle–Cardiff express. In its later years this locomotive carried two unofficial names — 'Queen 1' in September 1986 and 'Wyvern' from March 1987. Withdrawn on 27 April 1987, it would be stored for many years at March, finally being cut up at MC Metal Processing in February 1994. *Gavin Morrison*

Above: A Steam Locomotive Operators' Association (SLOA) Pullman special heads north past Goose Hill Junction, Normanton, leaving the since closed section of line from Oakenshaw, on 24 April 1983. On the left can be seen the signalbox (long since demolished) which controlled the junction where the ex-Midland and Lancashire & Yorkshire main lines merged. The locomotive is No 45 017 (ex-D23), another long-term Holbeck resident by now working from Tinsley. Withdrawn on 21 August 1985, it would pass into departmental stock as No ADB968024, based at Toton. This extended career would come to an end in January 1992, the locomotive finally being scrapped by MC Metal Processing in June 1993. *Gavin Morrison*

Right: The Leeds Holbeck fuelling shed can just be seen through the bridge on the left-hand side of the picture as No 45 073 (ex-D129), in immaculate condition, accelerates the 14.38 Leeds–Cardiff express south towards Sheffield on 13 September 1979. The locomotive enjoyed an eight-year allocation to Holbeck but would be withdrawn from Toton on 18 October 1981, being cut up by November 1982. *Gavin Morrison*

Left: No D134 (later No 45 076) stands on shed at Leeds Holbeck on 13 March 1962. The locomotive would be withdrawn on 12 November 1986 but not cut up (at MC Metal Processing, Glasgow) for a further seven years. *Gavin Morrison*

Right: Haulage of the 'Thames–Clyde Express' was dominated by the 'Peaks' for more than two decades. Here, on 25 May 1966, the down working passes Wortley Junction, Leeds, headed by one of Holbeck's Class 45s, No D20. Subsequently renumbered 45 013, this locomotive would be given two unofficial names — 'Queen 1' and later 'Wyvern' — by Tinsley depot towards the end of its career, being withdrawn in April 1987 although not cut up until February 1994, at MC Metals, Glasgow. *Gavin Morrison*

Right: The down 'Thames–Clyde Express', headed by No D12, races through the closed Newlay & Horsforth station, north of Leeds, on 11 June 1967. Note that the fast lines (on the right) are already out of use, the station having closed on 20 March 1965. Latterly numbered 45 011, this locomotive was another to spend many years allocated to Leeds Holbeck before being transferred to York. Withdrawn from Tinsley on 3 May 1981, it would be broken up by September 1981. *Gavin Morrison*

27

Left: Bingley Junction, at the north end of the Shipley Triangle, has altered progressively over the past 25 years, electrification being preceded by the installation of firstly a down and then an up platform. In the days before these changes, on 24 June 1976, No 45 012 (ex-D108) negotiates the sharp curve with a Nottingham–Glasgow train. Unofficially named 'Wyvern II' at Tinsley on 14 August 1987, the locomotive would be withdrawn on 27 July 1988, albeit not cut up until November 1992. *Gavin Morrison*

Above: In the days when Bradford Forster Square was served by trains from St Pancras as well as from the West Country No D106 passes Manningham station (closed since 20 March 1965) with a down express on 31 May 1966. In the background can be seen the old Midland Railway steam shed, which was to close the following year. No D106 would later be renumbered 45 106, in which guise it can be seen on page 7. *Gavin Morrison*

29

Left: A wintry scene in the Aire Valley as No 193 heads the up 'Thames–Clyde Express' (Glasgow St Enoch–St Pancras) between Steeton and Keighley on 16 February 1973. Latterly numbered 46 056, this locomotive was to spend its entire career allocated to the North East. Withdrawn on 31 October 1982, it would be cut up by the end of October 1985. *Gavin Morrison*

Above: No D117 was less than two months old when photographed heading a down express freight for Carlisle past Hellifield on 4 November 1961, before the application of yellow warning panels to locomotive ends. Later renumbered 45 130, it would be given the unofficial name 'Newmarket' at Tinsley shortly before withdrawal on 10 May 1987; five years would elapse before scrapping, at MC Metal Processing, Glasgow. *Gavin Morrison*

Left: Headed by No 45 150 (originally numbered D78 and briefly 45 054), the 16.37 Carlisle–Leeds passes Ribblehead station on 23 April 1984, the 10-coach train providing a marked contrast with today's two-car Class 156 DMU. Having received the unofficial name 'Vampire' at Tinsley on 18 August 1987, the locomotive would be withdrawn just over six months later, on 4 February 1988, ultimately being reduced to scrap by MC Metal Processing by December 1991. *Gavin Morrison*

Above: The most impressive feature of the Settle–Carlisle line is the 24-arch Ribblehead Viaduct, which is 104ft high and 440yd long. One of Leeds Holbeck's 'Peaks', No D17, heads the down 'Thames–Clyde Express' bound for Glasgow St Enoch on 11 October 1969. Latterly numbered 45 024, this locomotive would be withdrawn on 5 October 1980 and cut up in August 1983. *Gavin Morrison*

Above: Wintry conditions at England's highest station, Dent, on 15 February 1969 as the down 'Thames–Clyde Express' passes through on its way north, headed by No D25. Having spent 17 years allocated to Leeds Holbeck, the locomotive (by now renumbered 45 021) would be withdrawn from Tinsley depot on 14 December 1980 and cut up by April 1983. *Gavin Morrison*

Above right: Not the usual Holbeck 'Peak' but Derby-allocated No D102 heads the down 'Thames–Clyde Express' past Ais Gill Summit on 1 September 1962. As No 45 140 this locomotive would receive the unofficial name 'Mercury' at Tinsley on 25 July 1987; withdrawn on 29 March 1988, it would finally be cut up (by MC Metals) more than six years later, during June 1994. *Gavin Morrison*

Right: No D54 leaves Dumfries with the down working of the 'Thames–Clyde Express' in the early 1960s. The locomotive would be withdrawn (as No 45 023) on 12 September 1984 and cut up by November 1986. *Derek Cross*

Left: No 46 038 (ex-D175), seen leaving King's Cross with a relief for Edinburgh on 10 July 1976, was unusual in that it spent its entire career allocated to Gateshead. However, the majority of the Class 46s spent at least part of their lives allocated to this depot and as such were much more regular visitors to King's Cross than were the Class 45s. Withdrawn initially in December 1980 but later reinstated, No 46 038 would be finally withdrawn on 28 March 1982 and then stored at various locations, ultimately being cut up by November 1985. *Gavin Morrison*

Above: Heading south with an express for King's Cross, No 46 050 (ex-D187) passes Black Carr Junction, just south of Doncaster, on 30 January 1977, at which time there were no fewer than five signal gantries still in use. The locomotive was another Class 46 to spend its entire career allocated to Gateshead depot. Withdrawn in December 1980 but subsequently reinstated, it would be permanently retired on 31 October 1982, thereafter being stored at Healey Mills until removed for cutting up in February 1985. *Gavin Morrison*

37

Left: Doncaster Carr depot is just to the right of this picture of a very clean No 45 023 (ex-D54) *Lytham St Annes* hauling a loaded merry-go-round train on 26 March 1981. This locomotive achieved fame in September/October 1968, when, at Willington power station, its Sulzer power unit set a (then) world record for a diesel engine by running continuously for 341 hours. However, this distinction would not be enough to ensure its survival; withdrawn on 12 September 1984, it would be cut up by November 1986. *Gavin Morrison*

Above: Viewed from the high embankment at Beeston Junction, to the south of Leeds, No 45 102 (ex-D51) passes with the 10.48 Leeds City–Derby on 6 July 1975. The locomotive would be withdrawn on 11 September 1986 and cut up at Vic Berry's yard by December 1988. *Gavin Morrison*

39

Above: Since redeveloped as housing, the marshalling yard at Dringhouses, south of York, was still a hive of activity in 1977. In this view, recorded on 31 May that year, No 46 032 (ex-D169), in charge of a Newcastle–Cardiff train, has just overtaken Class 40 No 40059 (ex-D259) on a Newcastle–Liverpool express. The 'Peak' would be withdrawn at the end of April 1984, whereas the Class 40 would survive only until August 1977. *Gavin Morrison*

Right: A special about to change locomotives on the centre road under the fine roof of York station on 18 May 1974. No D101 has arrived from the south, while No 46 046 (recently renumbered from D183) is ready to take over for the journey to Scarborough. Renumbered 45 061, the former would be withdrawn on 16 August 1981, but No 46 046 would remain in service until 6 May 1984. *Gavin Morrison*

In the 1970s and early 1980s Scarborough provided plenty of variety on summer Saturdays. Here, on 2 August 1980, No 45 015 (ex-D14) prepares to leave with the 10.15 to Birmingham New Street. Having spent its first 17 years allocated to Leeds Holbeck, this locomotive would be withdrawn from Toton on 3 March 1986, later being moved to the Training Compound area. In 2002 it was sold for preservation to the Battlefield Line (near Market Bosworth), although, given its condition, restoration will be an expensive and lengthy task. *Gavin Morrison*

Class 46 No 46 030 (ex-D167) accelerates away from Darlington with a southbound cross-country express on the evening of 31 August 1975. The locomotive would be withdrawn on 26 October 1980 and cut up in November 1982. *Gavin Morrison*

Above: Heading along the very scenic section of the East Coast main line between Alnmouth and Burnmouth, No 46 027 (ex-D164) skirts the North Sea coast at Scremerston, three miles south of Berwick, with a cross-country train bound for Edinburgh on 10 June 1978. The locomotive would be withdrawn on 25 November 1984 and stored at Goole Docks, eventually being cut up at Vic Berry's Leicester yard by December 1986. *Gavin Morrison*

Right: A very clean No 46 040 (ex-D177) keeps company with Class 47 No 47 268, 'Deltic' No 55 018 *Ballymoss* and an unidentified Class 26 at Haymarket depot on 3 June 1978. The 'Peak' would be withdrawn on 14 December 1980 in order to yield much-needed spares for the rest of its class, being cut up by May 1982. *Gavin Morrison*

Above: Approaching St Austell station from the west No 45 003 (ex-D133) is seen slowing for a stop with the 13.54 working from Penzance on 6 September 1985. The locomotive would end its career on 9 December 1985 and be cut up at Vic Berry's of Leicester by March 1987. *Gavin Morrison*

Right: The 09.55 Penzance–Leeds passes Laira, Plymouth, accelerating hard before tackling the formidable 1-in-42 Hemerdon Bank, about two miles to the east, on 24 August 1985. The locomotive is No 45 132 (ex-D22), which would remain in service until 11 May 1987, eventually being sold (after almost five years in store at March) to the Mid-Hants Railway. *Gavin Morrison*

Above: No 45 030 (ex-D31) passes Aller Junction (to the west of Newton Abbot) with a down express before starting the climb to Dainton Summit on the evening of 11 August 1975. The locomotive would be withdrawn on 30 November 1980 and cut up by June 1981. Aller Junction too is no more, the junction for the Paignton and Plymouth lines now being located at Newton Abbot. *Gavin Morrison*

Right: At one of the most familiar locations in the UK for railway photography, No 23 (later No 45 017) pulls away from Teignmouth station, passing alongside the sea wall, with the up 'Devonian' on 30 August 1972. Withdrawn on 21 August 1985, the locomotive would pass into Departmental stock as No ADB968024, finally ending its career in January 1992 and being cut up in June 1993. *Gavin Morrison*

Left: Having paused for holidaymakers to alight, Bristol Bath Road-allocated No D143 (later No 46 006) departs from Dawlish on 2 September 1972. Withdrawn on 14 December 1980 following a period in store, this locomotive would be reinstated at Gateshead on 22 November 1981, finally ending its working days on 31 January 1982 but surviving for another 3½ years before being cut up. *Gavin Morrison*

Above: No 45 110 (ex-D73) had only recently received its new number when it was photographed passing through Dawlish Warren with a Summer Saturday working on 25 August 1973. The locomotive would gain the unofficial name 'Medusa' whilst allocated to its final depot, Tinsley, from where it would be withdrawn on 27 July 1988, ultimately being cut up in June 1990. *Gavin Morrison*

Above: This very fine picture, full of human interest (not to mention the signals and signalbox), was taken at the west end of Taunton station on 15 September 1979. The photographer, who was travelling on the 09.53 Sheffield–Paignton, headed by No 45 019 (ex-D33), had time to get off the train and grab this shot before resuming his journey to Exeter! Also heading for the West Country was No 46 038 (ex-D175) of Gateshead depot, whilst in the distance Class 47 No 47284 can be seen approaching with an up express. No 45 019 would be withdrawn on 4 September 1985 and cut up during December 1986, whilst No 46 038 would be withdrawn on 28 March 1982 (having been withdrawn once already and reinstated) and cut up by November 1985. *M. Mensing*

Right: No 46 047 (ex-D184) races through Bridgwater station on the long straight and virtually level section of line between Yatton and Cogload Junction with the 10.35 Leeds–Paignton on 12 April 1980. Remaining in service until 2 September 1984, the locomotive would be scrapped in January 1986. *M. Mensing*

Left: A heavy stone train headed by No 45 007 (ex-D119) heads east through Westbury station on 14 November 1979. The locomotive would bear the unofficial name 'Taliesin' from June 1987 whilst allocated to Tinsley, its final depot. Withdrawn 27 July 1988, it would not be scrapped until November 1992, at MC Metal Processing, Glasgow. *Gavin Morrison*

Above: Unofficially named 'Medusa' by Tinsley depot on 11 August 1987, No 45 110 (ex-D73) is shown in its final months of service, having just emerged from Twerton Tunnel, near Bath, with a down ballast train on 5 November 1987. It would be withdrawn 27 July 1988 and cut up on 13 June 1990 by MC Metals. *M. Mensing*

Above: Seen 1¼ miles south of the site of Laverton Halt (closed to passengers from 7 March 1960) on the Stratford-upon-Avon–Cheltenham line, onto which it had been diverted due to engineering work on the main line, No D20 (later No 45 013) heads west with the 07.32 Derby–Bristol Temple Meads on 15 May 1966. The locomotive was to spend its first 17 years allocated to Leeds Holbeck depot, before moving to York and then to Tinsley; withdrawn in April 1987, it would be broken up at MC Metals in February 1994. *M. Mensing*

Right: Another 'Peak' to spend the majority of its life (in this case its first 16 years, bar three months) allocated to Leeds Holbeck was No D27 (later No 45 028), seen on 3 May 1963 heading the 1.8pm Leeds City–Cardiff General past the site of Droitwich Road station (closed to passengers from 1 October 1855!), on the Worcester-avoiding route. The locomotive would be transferred in October 1977 to Tinsley; allocated there until withdrawn on 4 January 1981, it would be scrapped by April 1983. *M. Mensing*

Left: No 46 029 (ex-D166) spent its entire career allocated to either Holbeck or Gateshead and is pictured while working from the latter, passing King's Norton, in the Birmingham suburbs, with the 10.40 Manchester Piccadilly– Paignton on 21 May 1977. Withdrawn on 30 January 1983, it would be stored at various locations in the London area before arriving at Swindon, being eventually broken up there in September 1986. *M. Mensing*

Right: No 45 005 (ex-D79) passes Ryecroft Junction, near Walsall, with a bulk-cement working on 23 May 1978. This locomotive would be withdrawn on 17 March 1986, ending up at Vic Berry's scrapyard and being dismantled by 17 December 1988. *M. Mensing*

Below right: Still fitted with box-type headcodes, No 45 127 (ex-D87) heads a Newcastle-bound express through Burton-upon-Trent on 25 August 1980. Hard though it may be to believe today, formations of 10-12 coaches were the norm for the cross-country workings in the 1960s, '70s and '80s. Having sustained accident damage in May 1981, the locomotive would later receive the cab from No 45 047, thereafter remaining in traffic until 7 May 1987. Following storage at various locations, it would eventually be cut up at Gresty Lane, Crewe, by April 1994. *Gavin Morrison*

Left: Class 46 No 46 025 (ex-D162) approaches Whitchurch with the 10.00 Crewe–Cardiff on 22 September 1979. These passenger workings saw a wide variety of motive power in the 1970s and 1980s, including Class 25s, 33s, 37s, 46s, 47s and, in the early days, 'Warships' working through from the West Country. This locomotive was transferred to the Western Region in April 1971; retired initially on 14 December 1980 but reinstated at Gateshead, it would be withdrawn and reinstated again before finally ending its working days on 25 November 1984, ultimately being cut up in November 1985. *Gavin Morrison*

Above: Withdrawn on 14 December 1980 but reinstated on 22 November 1981, Gateshead-allocated Class 46 No 46 052 (ex-D189) heads an unidentified down express past the carriage sidings at the south end of Crewe station on 22 October 1983. This locomotive would finally end its working life in September 1984, albeit not scrapped until February 1986. *Gavin Morrison*

Ever since the West Coast main line was electrified north of Weaver Junction in 1974 diversions via Manchester have required diesel locomotives to haul the 'dead' electrics. Until Virgin Class 57/3s appeared in 2003 these duties were performed almost exclusively by Class 47s, so it was unusual to see No 45 101 (ex-D96) piloting Class 85 No 85 026 past the site of Manchester Exchange station at the head of the 07.10 Glasgow Central–Euston on 5 November 1983. Withdrawn on 13 November 1986 as a result of a main-generator burn-out at Darlington, No 45 101 would be cut up at Vic Berry's, Leicester, by October 1988. *Gavin Morrison*

In the days when there were still plenty of long-distance Summer Saturday extras to/from Blackpool, No 46 026 (ex-D163) *Leicestershire and Derbyshire Yeomanry* approaches Kirkham with the 12.30pm to Newcastle on 2 July 1983. The only Class 46 to be officially named, this locomotive spent around 19 years allocated to the Western Region but ended its career with a short spell at Gateshead, being withdrawn on 25 November 1984 and cut up by the end of March 1985. *Gavin Morrison*

Above: Having been largely ousted from their duties on the Midland main line in October 1982, the Class 45/1s became frequent performers on the trans-Pennine route via Diggle, on which some trains originated in North Wales. Glinting in the evening sunlight, No 45 115 (ex-D81) emerges from the Conwy Tubular Bridge as it approaches Llandudno Junction with a Bangor–York train on the evening of 19 September 1986. Towards the end of its career unofficially named 'Apollo' by Tinsley depot, this locomotive would be withdrawn on 13 June 1988 and cut up in June 1990. *Gavin Morrison*

Right: No 45 114 (ex-D94) passes through Deganwy station on 20 September 1986 at the head of the 15.16 Llandudno–York. Remaining in service until 17 February 1987, this locomotive would survive for another seven years before being cut up at MC Metal Processing, Glasgow. *Gavin Morrison*

Left: No 46 016 (ex-D153) prepares to enter the deep cutting at Olive Mount, Liverpool, with the 14.05 Liverpool–Scarborough trans-Pennine express on 11 September 1982. This locomotive was unusual for a Class 46 in that during the course of its career it was allocated to the London Midland, Western, North Eastern and (briefly) Scottish regions. Latterly given the unofficial name of 'Oscar', it would be withdrawn on 31 December 1983 and scrapped in September 1984. *Gavin Morrison*

Above: Wintry conditions in the Pennines on 22 February 1986 as No 45 143 (ex-D62) heads the 12.05 Liverpool–Scarborough past Diggle just before entering the 5,344yd Standedge Tunnel. Named *5th Royal Inniskilling Dragoon Guards* at St Pancras station on 30 November 1964, the locomotive would be withdrawn on 7 May 1987, albeit not cut up until March 1994. *Gavin Morrison*

Left: The morning Newcastle–Liverpool train passes through the deep cutting at Paddock, just to the west of Huddersfield, on the 1-in-105 climb to Marsden, on 14 June 1979. In charge is Gateshead's No 46 046 (ex-D183), which would return with the afternoon working. The locomotive would be withdrawn on 5 May 1984 and cut up by November 1985. *Gavin Morrison*

Above: No 45 133 (ex-D40) emerges from the tunnel at Huddersfield and into the station, heading a Liverpool–Scarborough express on 8 August 1986. It would be withdrawn from Tinsley on 11 May 1987 and then stored at various locations before being purchased for preservation and restored to working order at the Midland Railway Centre, Butterley. *Gavin Morrison*

Above: When engineering work takes place on the trans-Pennine Standedge route traffic is diverted via the Calder Valley. Here, on 13 October 1985, No 45 112 (ex-D61) *Royal Army Ordnance Corps* heads past the site of Elland station (closed from 10 September 1962) with an express for Liverpool. Withdrawn on 7 May 1987, the locomotive would be sold in 1991 to the East Lancashire Railway. Restored to working order, in June 1999 it was re-sold to Fragonset Railways and can thus once again be seen running on the national rail network. Plans to reopen a station at Elland have yet to bear fruit, however. *Gavin Morrison*

Above right: Photographed on 9 May 1966, No D168 heads a Newcastle–Liverpool express past the steam shed at Mirfield, which was to close the following year.

Apart from three months at Holbeck in 1972 this locomotive was to spend its entire career (latterly as No 46 031) allocated to Gateshead, being a frequent performer on trans-Pennine workings. Withdrawn in April 1983, it would be cut up in August of that year. *Gavin Morrison*

Right: Headed by No 45 111 (ex-D65) *Grenadier Guardsman*, the 12.05 Liverpool–Newcastle crosses the River Calder as it approaches Mirfield station on 8 May 1982. The locomotive would be withdrawn on 7 May 1987 and moved to various sites, including the Railway Technical Centre at Derby, finally being cut up in July 1992. *Gavin Morrison*

Above: No 45 138 (ex-No D92) heads a diverted trans-Pennine express for Liverpool past the cement terminal to the east of Dewsbury, where today the company Locotec repairs and hires out diesel locomotives, some of which are ex-BR. Photographed on 7 September 1986, the train would rejoin its normal route at Thornhill Junction, a couple of miles further on. Withdrawn on 22 December that year, the locomotive would not be cut up until March 1994. *Gavin Morrison*

Right: Heading for Healey Mills yard with a train of empty spoil wagons, an immaculate No 45 053 (ex-D76) passes the site of the former Horbury & Ossett station on 27 April 1977. The locomotive was obviously ex-Derby Works but at this stage still retained its headcode boxes. Stored in December 1979, it would be sent for refurbishing in January 1983, but this was not to be, the locomotive being officially withdrawn on 27 November 1983 and eventually cut up at Crewe in October 1988. *Gavin Morrison*

Left: Seen from above the entrance to Morley Tunnel (3,369yd), an unidentified 'Peak' passes Morley Low station at the head of the morning Newcastle–Liverpool express on 23 June 1975. *Gavin Morrison*

Above: Headed by No D186, the 10.00 Liverpool Lime Street–Newcastle emerges from Marsh Lane Cutting, Leeds, and passes Neville Hill depot on 8 June 1967. The locomotive appears to be painted in a slightly lighter shade of blue than that used subsequently and also has red buffer-beams. Later renumbered 46 049, it would be withdrawn on 12 December 1982, eventually being cut up by October 1985. *Gavin Morrison*

Left: No D15 (later No 45 018) spent 17 years working from Leeds Holbeck depot. In this picture, taken on 10 June 1967, it is heading a down van train, probably to Bradford Forster Square, into the deep cutting at Rodley, to the north of Leeds. Note that the locomotive has nose-end doors and inside corridor connections, Nos D11-15 being the only production 'Peaks' so fitted. This locomotive would end its days at Tinsley, being withdrawn on 4 January 1981 and broken up by the end of October 1982. *Gavin Morrison*

Right: Locomotive-hauled passenger workings into Bradford Interchange are nowadays very rare. In happier times, on Sunday 29 July 1979, No 46 011 (ex-D148) leaves with the 16.50 for Birmingham and tackles the 1-in-50 climb to St Dunstans. This locomotive would be withdrawn on 25 November 1984 and broken up in January 1986. *Gavin Morrison*

Above: Nameplate of No 45 104 (ex-D59).

Above right: Name of No 45 135 (ex-No D99) as painted on by Tinsley depot staff, complete with shedcode.

Right: Nameplate of No 45 044 (ex-D63).

Below right: Nameplate of No 45 041 (ex-D53).

Bottom right: Nameplate of No 45 046 (ex-D68), minus regimental badge.

Below: Replacement nameplate of No 45 104 (ex-No D59) as applied by Tinsley depot staff.

All the 'Peak' classes are well represented in preservation, their ranks comprising two Class 44s, three Class 45/0s, nine Class 45/1s and three Class 46s. Today only Nos 45 112 and 46 035 are certified to run on Network Rail, although many are in operational condition on various preserved lines. Representing the preserved locomotives, No 4 *Great Gable* is pictured working a Rawtenstall–Bury train on the East Lancashire Railway during a diesel gala on 7 July 1998. *Gavin Morrison*

No D172 was delivered new on 2 July 1962 to Gateshead depot, where it spent its entire career, latterly as No 46 035, until withdrawn from normal service on 25 November 1984. It then moved to the Railway Technical Centre, being transferred to Departmental stock as No 97 403 and used to haul Research Department test trains. Named *Ixion* at Toton depot in May 1985, the locomotive was withdrawn again on 19 August 1991, eventually (in January 1993) being sold to Pete Waterman, who financed restoration to full working order in green livery.

Prior to receiving its main-line certificate it spent some time undergoing tests at Tinsley depot, where it is seen on 11 January 1994. After a long and expensive overhaul it would eventually receive its main-line certificate in August, working its first train from Derby to St Pancras — an historic first run on BR metals by a preserved diesel — on Saturday 1 October 1994; the following day it hauled the 'Thames–Clyde Express' special from St Pancras to Sheffield and return, performing faultlessly throughout. *Gavin Morrison*